Darlene Young's writing coll
earth, shows us the glory-wr
These aren't poems. The

—James Goldberg
author of *The Five Books of Jesus*

Darlene Young shows us what it means to "carry a landscape in [our] blood." Her wise (and often snarky) poems are introspective gems that elevate the ordinary and revel in the paradoxes of everyday Mormon life. More importantly, they remind us what it means belong and seek belonging in a community of Saints. These are poems that speak to the Mormon heart as well as the Mormon heartland. *Homespun and Angel Feathers* is a gift for anyone who has ever gazed "across a weed-scrabbled/mountain valley" and yearned for home.

—Scott Hales
author of *The Garden of Enid: Adventures of a Weird Mormon Girl*

Darlene Young's poems celebrate the beauty, humor, and pathos of everyday life in wise and surprising ways. She is unafraid to explore the depth and breadth of familiar subjects, locating the divine in the mundane, exploding the myth that in order to live deliberately, the poet must go out into the woods, alone. Surrounded by a houseful of teenagers, grappling with the demands of middle age, confronting health problems, balancing church and professional responsibilities, simply getting the dishes done—it is in the midst of all of this lived experience that Young stops and takes note. Suffused with crackling language and precise imagery, her poetry helps us stop and take note as well.

—Angela Hallstrom
author of *Bound on Earth*
and editor of *Dispensation: Latter-day Fiction*

Although *Homespun and Angel Feathers* is Darlene Young's first book, it seems to be the work of a long-published, successful poet. Young is a wise and seasoned woman who knows herself and what matters to her, and who has studied seriously to perfect her craft. In this collection, she succeeds at some of poetry's most difficult tasks: it is much more challenging to affirm than to negate; it is many degrees harder to express faith than to express doubt; much greater skill is required to write successfully of daily family life rather than of the bizarre or extraordinary. Darlene Young does all these things exquisitely. Her tone is frank, down-to-earth, quirky, as if she is indeed the Lord's "holy kazoo." Because she is honest about the struggles and disagreements of family life, she is entirely believable when she also writes of her love for her husband and sons. Her poems embody the emotions she hopes to share with the reader; she describes one son's "still narrow shoulders, crooked / tie," another's "granola and earphones," marriage as "the nubby recliner in the corner," and daily life as "torque and tonnage." Because Young has spent time with her language, has carefully explored its connotations as well as its aural and imaginative possibilities, her greatest achievement is to write originally about her faith. She is decidedly a Latter-day Saint writing to other Latter-day Saints, with poems about the prophet Joseph, Adam and Eve, the temple, and church life. *Homespun and Angel Feathers* is a bright new star in the ever-expanding galaxy of Mormon poetry.

—Susan Howe
author of *Salt*, associate editor of BYU Studies,
and winner of the Association for Mormon Letters
Lifetime Achievement Award

"Home-made, home-made! But aren't we all?" These words, from Elizabeth Bishop's "Crusoe in England," seem a fitting intro to this charming debut collection. The world Darlene Young observes is cobbled-together, strange, a bit wobbly—fallen but irresistibly so. Her chief tools are romanticism and irony, which she juggles with skill. The result? Poems that are both sassy and sacred, holy and hungry—poems, in short, that praise. "I'll be your holy kazoo," she says to God on page one. And we, lucky readers, eavesdrop for the rest of the collection.

—Lance Larsen
Utah poet laureate, 2012–17

Darlene Young's poetry consistently delights and surprises. She can evoke tears and chuckles—sometimes within one poem.

This book is a gift and an invitation to receive more gifts. Young unfolds new perspectives and insights on Biblical texts, the miraculous messiness of motherhood, the challenges and blessings of being a woman of faith in a demanding, noisy world, and the triumphant dimensions of love.

Darlene Young's poetry should be read re-read, savored, shared.

—Margaret Blair Young
past president of the Association for Mormon Letters
and author of *I am Jane*

Homespun and Angel Feathers

BY COMMON CONSENT PRESS is a non-profit publisher dedicated to producing affordable, high-quality books that help define and shape the Latter-day Saint experience. BCC Press publishes books that address all aspects of Mormon life. Our mission includes finding manuscripts that will contribute to the lives of thoughtful Latter-day Saints, mentoring authors and nurturing projects to completion, and distributing important books to the Mormon audience at the lowest possible cost.

Homespun and Angel Feathers

Poetry by
Darlene Young

BCC
PRESS

For information contact
By Common Consent Press
4062 S. Evelyn Dr.
Salt Lake City, UT 84124-2250

Cover design: Mikey Brooks
Book design: Andrew Heiss

www.bccpress.org

ISBN-10: 1-948218-17-8
ISBN-13: 978-1-948218-17-7

10 9 8 7 6 5 4 3 2 1

For my mother,
Sharla Jane Eldredge Luker (1949–1993), who,
though always yearning, was always singing,

and for her mother,
Jane Ludwig Eldredge (1928–1962), who,
though I never met her in this life,
planted poetry in my blood.

Contents

Then we are fierce and holy;
then we are wild and wise.

                          —Marvin Payne

Glory be to God for dappled things

                          —Gerard Manley Hopkins

"Lord, Make Me an Instrument of Thy Peace"

OK, let's get this straight. When I said it,
I meant *tool*. Tackle, widget, implement, device.
Something cool and sharp with important work to do:
a screwdriver, maybe. Scalpel or forceps.
Ophthalmoscope. I would have settled for tweezers,
chopstick—heck, even a toothpick has its dignity and place
(raspberry seed, lunch with the boss).

Or, if we're thinking music, how about a harp
or piano? I could pluck and finger thy word
for the world. But I'm clumsy; I get that. Then
why not go large, with chimes, or a kettle drum?
Or a sassy trumpet, blazing with thy breath?
Sure, I'm not gong-strong, nor flute pure, but maybe
I could be bagpipes—or viola, the plain older sister?

Moving into middle age, I begin to see the joke
and joy of what you've made of my life: yes,
your breath has been in me, and on days
I manage to flatten myself thin enough,
translucent as waxed paper, I vibrate,
resonant in your wind. You humming through me:
curious timbre. Ticklish, tangy, and strange;
good enough. I'll be your holy kazoo. Selah.

Singing Lesson

She says I should croak,
whine, yowl, get out
of the way, turn
myself inside out.
She says, "Lie
on the floor." For support,
she claims, but really
it's to shrink me.
I'm a learner of a new
language, a baby babbling
with delight in the flight
of her own voice. I suck
my belly up, sneer
my cheeks and shriek.
"It's mechanical,
not personal," she says,
so I try to disappear into the punch
of each note kathunking
down the scales like luggage
on stairs. It takes guts,
and faith. I want to sing
beauty into the world, that trite

old egotistical dream of being
a conduit, a resonation
with God's creation like
the perfect overtone of a stone
cathedral, like a knowing
look from across a room
or the taking of a feverish child
into my arms. But it seems
that jagged precedes smooth,
at first; brashness and sass
trump grace. Breathe
deep, open up. Crow.

Woman

As a girl I drank
the sky danced
barefoot on grass
my skin without border
my body a flute
for God's laughter.
Enough: to meet
each morning fully
awake hit the pillow
reluctantly and hard.

Older I sucked
what light I could
through cloth glanced
sideways slouched.
My skin couldn't hide me
enough my body
a dandelion too garish
at first then blown
about the yard its root
burdensome and blunt.

Older I drained
myself into other mouths
wringing I wished
to abound glorious
in my wild prodigal
plenty plummy
and ripe but fear
made me miserly
counting the costs.

What happens to a girl
at fifteen? at thirty?
What taught me to
hold back hoard
and scrimp knot
my body into a hard tool?

Older I'm nearing my
crone-hood; now
that no one asks I'll give.
Let me sink my ugly
beautiful root deep
drink the world unfurl
my shameless petals
to the sky blousy
and plush.

Shepherds

Don't tell me about rose-cheeked Arcadian youth
gathering daisies on a hillside
piping tunes to their cloud-fluffy sheep
under the stars.

No, these were foul-smelling, lusty
men with dirty necks, greasy hands;
snorting, arguing, joke-telling, nose-picking
men—one wearing stolen
sandals (although I admit he felt
guilty about it)—gambling on who
had the best aim as they chucked rocks
at a nearby lizard.

You talk about salt of the earth!
These men were salty, alright,
downright ornery, some of them,
fighting sometimes and yelling
at their wives when they were home,
which wasn't often.

Yeah, I'll grant you Dan
was an innocent
and Dave had some noble moments
and none of them was really evil
but they all had dirty fingernails
of one kind or another
when the light came—

yes, it came.
But don't take away that moment just before—
flies whining over the sheep dung
and Jake and Zeke having a
spitting contest—
that's the key moment, you see,
in all their grimy glory;

it has to be.

Because the light came to me, too.
Allelujah.

Kintsukuroi for Joseph Smith

Planted in farmdirt and manure, he faced eternity
and translated for us. Meeting of meat and light,
bucket, shovel, axe transubstantiated. Receiver,
transmitter, amplifier, he would bring us with him,
modulate us to a higher key. Yes, he was rough,
the course coupling, the intersection of dimensions
dirty and divine, the rustic needle on the holy
phonograph. But I can forgive the static;
who wants a perfect prophet? Hick and height,
scrub and scripture, limp and lamp, he was a handshake
with the heavens (callused hands, constellations unnumbered),
matter and antimatter. Not immaterial
his fumble and slop, his gimpy stuttering lope towards loft.
I need his lusty, sloppy flaws; I am drab and itch myself.
I prefer a dusty plough. I'll make my home here
among the homespun and angel feathers.

Angels of Mercy

The Seventh Ward Relief Society
presidency argued long and soft
whether Janie Goodmansen deserved
to have the sisters bring her family meals.
It seemed that precedent was vague—
no one was sure if "boob job" qualified
as a legitimate call for aid.
Janie herself had never asked for help—
a fault they found harder to forgive
even than the vanity behind
the worldliness of D-cup ambition.
But in the end charity did not fail.
The sisters marched on in grim duty
each evening clutching covered casseroles
(for, after all, it wasn't the children's fault).
More than once, though, by some oversight
the dessert came out a little short, as if
by some consensus they all knew
that Janie's husband, Jim, could do
without a piece of pie that night.

Echo of Boy

My son hunches into the storm in his oversized coat
to collect fast offerings, a two-hour route
because the other mothers' sons stay in when it's cold.
He is mine.
His wrists

out-hang his sleeves. His hair
squirms from his well-slicked part,
and he is mine. He's out there
in the snow and I can't settle. Thirteen years old; thirteen,

    the way he slides a little to the right of us on the Sunday pew,
    like someone has hit "tab" on the keyboard, though still
       he'll let me pull him back to drape my arm around
       those slumping shoulders.
       Shadow of boy.

    It's snowing and he is fine out there.
    He's fine. At home
    he sprawls on the couch behind those heavy eyes. Outline
of boy. Echo of boy. I tell it to him straight: "The reward
for showing up," I say, "is that you're the first one they call
next time. Find a way to be proud of that." He looks
      away. Should I apologize for this burden of duty I've bred
      into him, for the fact that from now on he'll leave
      no ward gathering without putting away chairs? Welcome
      to Mormon guilt, my son. Welcome to the wilderness.
      Sometimes a suit is a front bumper, silver plating,
        deadweight.

Sometimes it is wings.

Those heavy-lidded eyes. Let there be a man
behind there. The still-narrow shoulders, crooked
tie. Does he slump to parenthesize the space
    he'll leave when he's gone? Look
    forward, son. Look forward,
    mother. On the horizon
    in the chalky dusk:
        contrail of boy.

Utah Mormon

The people you want for employees
but not friends. Big families
too shiny for belief—we must
be paper dolls. Look at me: I'm heavy
books, white teeth, organ music
and casseroles, but I crank
up the radio in my car same
as you, scream at God
sometimes, haul myself
bedraggled through awkward
misunderstandings. Half of me
fears you see me as wacko;
half of me knows you don't
see me at all. Still, I'll smile
my big white teeth. I'm the suit
and the dress, spires and spurs.
I am my people, bonneted,
ancient, dusty as sage,
but tangy. Let me get close
and you'll hear the shiver
of juniper, the cricket's
dry thrum. I carry

a landscape in my blood, brown
haunted by green. Scrub oak
fringes my dreams, and out there,
across a weed-scrabbled
mountain valley, the cottonwood
advertises a riverbed, probably dry.
Always the possibility of a house
sheltered there, always at a distance.
I never arrive. The longing
becomes the destination, sweet
in its way. Without the motion
I'd be bereft: Eve stuck
forever in a garden going
nowhere. Mormon
is the horizontal of the flinty earth,
the vertical of spires. Every year
a camp-out; every year the farm.
We can't escape the land
but it is never an end.
Permanent nostalgia, a home
made of homesickness.

Frodo Escorts Us to the Campground Via Audiobook

This is happening.
This is happiness.

—Robert Penn Warren

We're all cramped in the minivan. Something is happening—I know because Peter has stopped kicking the back of my seat. Outside is the scenery of southern Utah, the long stretches between national parks: scrub oak, sage, pinion pine, gray sky; away from the highway, farmhouses sheltered by cottonwoods. My sons' stillness makes the hair on my neck rise. In the rearview, I see their profiles, eyes on the distance. They are with Legolas, squinting at the horizon to see armies approaching. They were angry at me this morning when I forbade them from bringing the dvd player on the trip. Only their bodies are here, and I love them so dearly for being absent, for being on that plain with Legolas. Eyes open, ears even more fully open.

Here, now, is the smell of pretzels, fruit snack wrappers in the drink-holders, granola bar crumbs on the floor. Jon has forgotten to complain about Peter's pillow nudging into his space. In an hour, his head will be on his brother's shoulder, and his brother won't complain because Frodo is tempted once again to put on the ring. The sun is going down and the mountains in the east are tipped pink. Tonight we'll pull into the campsite and the boys will jump out to help crank up the camper. When we're all settled inside in our sleeping bags, they'll ask me to read a little from the book, but I'll pick a different one so that we can resume Frodo's story in the car tomorrow. One of them will be asleep before the third page, but the other will have beautiful wide eyes, blurring as he gazes at the lantern, which will dim gradually when I turn it off, and I will glide into my own starry dreams. They will dream of quests, and I will dream of their fraying denim knees and the hair in their eyes. I will dream of the smell of their napes when they were babies. I will dream of them leaving me someday.

Horizon

> *A girl puts her head on a boy's shoulder;*
> *they are driving west.*
>
> —*Galway Kinnell*

The cool tangerine sky.
Outside Wells, Nevada, a belt blows.
They have their whole lives ahead of them.

At the garage, the mechanic listens to classical music.
5 hours to kill in the killing heat.
She will have a bout with breast cancer at 58.

They walk around town, game for adventure.
Storage units, Check-n-Loan, acupuncture.
One of their children will break their hearts.

He could get a tattoo while she gets her nails done.
A boy throws a rubber ball against the parking-lot barrier.
Dog pens in the trailer park.

Hardware store: drawer-pulls and doorbells. Beef jerky, car air
    fresheners.
He tries on cowboy hats.
At 72, he will begin his slide into Alzheimer's. She will brush his
    teeth.

Somewhere, someone is practicing a clarinet.
The mechanic offers them tomatoes from his garden.
They pull out at dusk, her hand out the window, arcing and diving.

The stars, the sage. They could be anywhere.
Their carpet will turn powdery and dank. There will be grandbabies.
The cool of the earth, tangerine.

Twenty miles south of Malad, Idaho

is nothing. The stubbled, scrubby hills roll
away from the freeway like a lover who has lost
interest. Look: here and there, a stubborn pioneer
of a tree points to God, whose face fills the sky
looking absent. Sensing it, people drive
with their heads down, bent
to the task of arriving. But it's velvety dusk.
Let's take our time.

Farmhouse windows come on like lighthouses
in the wide dark. Inside them, people floss
their teeth, read comics to each other, tell
their teenagers to turn it off. Imagine
knocking on a door out there, being invited
by a farmer's wife from the 1950s
into a house of flowered curtains, clean
sheets. She would offer us warm milk,
and there would be a dog.

One time I made this drive on my own, eight-and-a-half
months pregnant. During these long stretches, I wanted to hold
my breath: my babies come fast. Though I planned to head back
  first
thing the next morning, I awoke in labor, which lasted
only an hour. If, if. If labor had delayed just three hours,
I would have delivered in the dust.

Let's map it out: just here I might feel that crushing
urgency. No hospital for an hour either direction. What
would you do? Could you find that farmhouse, that soft-
armed woman? Or would you keep driving, try

to make it to the one truck stop out here
(we passed it ten miles back), become familiar
with those dirty tiles, the faucet that runs
constantly and only cold?

For the first three months, every time I nursed my baby
(would we have named him Malad?) I thought
of this gravel shoulder, that sagebrush. I bet the greasy-
haired high-school dropout cashier
who would have brought me paper towels
lives in one of those houses. She is the daughter
the mother prays over every night, wishing she'd come home early
for the warm milk.

The Guys I Didn't Marry

The guys I didn't marry have hairy backs and need to lose a few pounds. They never vacuum their cars. They have peanut allergies.

The guys I didn't marry look pretty good for their age. They dream about flying, or about eating meatballs.

Every seven years or so, they dream of me.

The guys I didn't marry have become dj's and live in their parents' garages. They forget to take their meds. Regularly, they stub their toes on the porch step.

The guys I didn't marry run a marathon every year. They skinny-dip at Lake Powell with their lovers.

At least six times in the past two years, they have experienced moments of unbearable happiness.

The guys I didn't marry thank their lucky stars they didn't marry me. Most of them think they broke my heart, or that they never really loved me after all and were just caught up in the moment.

Some of them married the next girl they kissed.

The guys I didn't marry have a hard time throwing away their ratty underwear. They ignore current events.

They wait in line.

Some of the guys I didn't marry wept at the end of *Lord of the Rings*. At night, they stare at the ceiling. Most of them can't understand their fathers-in-law.

The guys I didn't marry pull out moldy drywall after they discover the slow leak. They whistle while they work—mostly Oingo Boingo, but some Phil Collins. They do the cooking but don't wash the pans.

They take their wives on cruises. They fly kites with their daughters, and their golden retrievers run in the sun and bark with joy.

All of them have low-back pain.

Account

I understand year after year
doing a few same things
in the same house with the same person
settled and unsettled, in for the long haul
                    —Stephen Dunn

Since I met you, the minutes I've spent
        wondering what was meant by a   kiss or
a look. The preparations on days I'll see you: make-up,
        those shoes. The hunt, the bait, the   catch and
being caught. Then the happy celebration of our   release
        from the chase, the plans made in the   park and
the car and the store and the office: whirligig joy-   ride
        wedding. Settling in. Working it out. Having to   chew and
worry the places that rub each other raw: what we can   swallow
        on behalf of the other. Where we will   live and
        whose parents' for Thanksgiving? The trick: to   let live
in our new garden what was our separate best, but   search and
        clear a space for what is new growth.
                Time to kneel in the dirt and   rescue
tender shoots from the snails. The learning not to   nip and
pick at the sore spots. Dropping the subject. The   tuck
of the sheet or a curl behind the ear, a foot-rub. The   give and
        lean of the dance. List it all out, and the final   take-
                away: you're costly. But knowing
                this wouldn't have made me   duck. And
        I've got fifty more years or so to invest.
                Sign me up. Let me dis-   cover
        more ways to burn minutes with you.

Salt

Grandpa weeps   and your hand
on my back is like shade   I think
while rubbing his feet of the tuck
and purl of   yourlegsandmine
when we finally climb into bed
after the mountain of today
   after all the mountains of all our days

you are my yellow bicycle you
are my dusk   the oh of the space of your name
in my mouth   the child with a jar
full of grass   we
will get old we will pleach
melting into each other like limp
lettuce losing its borders

you
are the salt to me you
   are the tinge and the glint and
I'll always turn my head to catch you I see
your handwriting
on the backs of my eyelids   your voice
is my blanket the kitten in the shrubs when the gutter
swells with cigarette butts

in the ebbing of the tide we cling
to the pilings   cobwebs and morning glory
   afterimage
if you exit before me
I'll dwindle like Grandpa
   a ring around the bathtub   a book-
mark on the floor

First Marriage

Eve walks in beauty.
Eve's natural state
is forward motion,
grace in the walking.

Adam's natural state:
a Barca-lounger ("Bring me a drink,
would you, Babe?").
But that's a holy place, too,
the holding still
inside beauty,
grace in the being.

Eve says, "What's next?"
She wants to bound
forward, abound,
magnify—
what is God
but continual progress,
forward motion?

Adam says, "Wait!
Look around you.
What is God
but continual presence,
immoveable?"

Grab hands.
Motion in presence,
presence in motion:
dance.

Digestion in the Garden

Cherries and pears, pomegranates, peaches
apricot syrup that zings through the bloodless
veins, courses down to your Achilles and back again
to the dancing heart still cycling backwards.
Parsley, asparagus, kumquat and kiwi
and sometimes potato for big belly sleepiness.

Enough, if you can learn to love the yearning,
trust the manna, never hoard. Call it good,
sweet aching empty, then the filling, then the spending—
like the tides, like the branches waving in the wind.
Wax, coil, spring, dance, rejoice.
wane, wink, yawn, bend, breathe.

Enough, a pleasant peaceful place. But
here's a stranger saying maybe there's a way
to do without the yearning, satisfy it once
and for all, achieve in one bite the end,
reach your destination.

(Didn't even know you were on a journey.)

Now you catch
a glimmer of the path beneath your feet:
appetite, imagination, expectation, lust
for all that's good—and how can it be wrong
to have it, whatever it is, ingest, digest,
become, arrive, achieve, be full?

Didn't God plant the hunger and the tree?

Now you sit and sigh against the tree
in momentary satiety, feel the changing of your heart
as bubbly spirit turns to muddy blood under your skin
that pools around your still digesting gut and
wakes a new and gnawing lust for meat,
wakes a fear of cold and thirst and death,

wakes, with growing horror and with joy,
a mind to see that yes, it was a lie, and yet
it was a truth as well: there is a destination;
there is a path.

First Meat

They already knew "knife,"
that-which-makes-fruit-fit-in-the-mouth,
but the angel had to teach them "fire,"
rough-bark-light-dance. The cutting
of the wood led

to Adam's first "pain" (deep-bitterherb-bite)
and "blood" (earth-water-dark-bringer),
but not Eve's,
having known her first menstruation
(life-death-marker)
since the day after the banishment.

The light from the knife in the sun seared their eyes.

The squeal of the lamb when they caught it,
then its scream
as Adam's angel-guided hand drew the knife—

a new sound for this new place.

The angel wept.
The angel said, "Think of another pain,
the pain of a father for his son."

They did not know that they would know
what he meant soon enough.

"Thorns, Briars, and Noxious Weeds"

I didn't know it meant *you*, the lady at work,
the saccharine rural accent and big hair, the burnt-egg gossip
by which you scribble boredom in the over-cooled air
of our endless, snarling buzz-saw days together.
I am meant to love you. I am meant
to picture an invisible pain inside you, the cause
of your caustic smalltalk, snide gratings and whines.
But I can't. I picture you as a high-mileage Buick with
bald tires, pitiful and heavy and still moving.
I picture you lonely. It doesn't help.
Daily I bark my shins on your edginess. Why can't I break
your orbit, scrabble free from your tack? The world
is like this. The world
is a gunky barbecue, a sagging bumper, fretting dogs
in the distance, hangnails and scraped palms, splinters
in the skin. I signed up for this
when I ate that fruit back in the garden—
that boring, gentle garden.
I hadn't known that *this* would be the adventure,
this torque and tonnage of dailiness, leaden and dull.
Intermittent toxin; sporadic sublime.
Looks like the only way back to the garden
is to harrow it out here between us,
my accidental guru, my vivifying thorn.

Morning Limp

1.

Still life with toast. This rich schtick:
a love-limp square dance for a clammy family.
Something seeps out through the skylight,
the refrigerator door. If we're lucky,
there is the slant of flocked smalltalk.
We finally get rolling and the chain falls
off the bike. An intake of breath, a quiet
rampage. Missing the context, mis-
matching socks. Can't wrestle past
the blather: dropped eyes, dropped
subjects. We're south of peace, east
of rest. Someone shake this snowglobe.

2.

You, my once-pink once-baby sprawl
over the table, gritty granola and earphones,
all shades drawn. Elvis has left the building.
I concentrate my glow:
does the back of your neck feel warm?
Strung long in this mortar and pestle morning
routine I load the washer: permanent press,
the vertical line between my eyebrows.
Don't remember me this way.
My catechism of duty is occasionally interrupted
by the stunning forked flash
of you: the suddenly broad back, the snort
at a joke you didn't used to get.
Not sure whether it's you or my picture of you
that I love, though I'm sure it's love.

3.
We drive to the high school.
The opal of your heavy-
lidded eyes. Behind them:
empty buildings, manila
envelopes. Your hair in your eyes
like wet mittens and woodsmoke.
Your paprika freckles, leaves
in the gutter. The windshield
smeared with the crust
of what I said when I meant
something else.   I meant:
you, alone in the wind,
chasing something. Chafed.
I meant: forgive me. How
hate can fog a windshield.
Your baggy clothes steam.

4.
Your hair in your eyes. You duck
when I reach to rumple it, ogre
that I am. Where
are the galoshes for navigating
this reedy wetland? Fe, fi, fo, fumble.
Our lines cross but on parallel planes.
Look: from the right angle
we look like we meet.

Frequencies

Today when I cut you off in traffic
accidentally I wished I had a horn,
a separate horn like Harpo Marx,
one whose sound was universally
acknowledged to mean "Mea Culpa,"
to mean "Forgive me." Mostly to mean
"Don't hate me." We should all have them.
We could give them to teenagers to carry
in the halls at school (or maybe that's what eyelash
extensions are for?). We could install
them surgically, make them involuntary,
like tails. Watch the twitch of the tail
of a stalking cat: a cat can't lie. What if
we couldn't either? All the guile gone.
Would we flutter like bats dodging
against each other's sincerity, resort
to autistic spinning to tune out
all the pathos bouncing around? Someone
would invent a cream to block 80%
of the damaging rays—though, of course,
a smartphone does just as well.

To a Red Traffic Light

In my simulated leather coinpurse
of moments, yours are the paperclips,
the lint stuck to the Velcro, enameled
trinkets. I check for lipstick on my teeth,
do my Kegels. Some kisses I owe
to you, snagged with one eye open
in case I missed your passing. Used
to be I was young enough to glance
around hoping someone was glancing around
for me. Time-machine, you turn me seventeen
when I crank up the volume and dance,
seventy when my kids see me and wince.
The rearview mirror is a scrapbook,
children sleeping like peaches
in carseats, teenagers gazing at traffic
while baring their souls. You make
of the windows a fake-walnut frame
for a suburban montage: loping
dogs, jogging housewives, wheelchairs,
elderly crossing guards. People
who pound their steering wheels, people
who weep. Nothing was ever a truer
mirror of a self unconstructed;
you'll be subpoenaed at the pearly gates.
You are the semicolons in my life, a pause
to feel my age. The place where I miss
my mother. A discotheque of ghosts.

Chronic

It's seeping sickly at the edge of things,
this winter I watch rotting from my bed.
Graveled gray with mottled car exhaust,
snow lurks in grizzled scabby patches. Dead
and graying grass lies matted underneath,
a lumpy mattress under twisted sheets.
A flagpole chain is gnawing at the wind.
The heavy brownish sky covers the peaks
that just last autumn jeweled the sky. Still,
I know they're up there, looking down like God
presiding over righteous-angled streets.
My furnace rumbles on. A wretched dog
malingers down my street towards afternoon.
It tells me there is no such thing as *soon*.

How Long?

I find myself Lehi, encamped in a tent.
It's pleasant enough here, with plenty to do.
Arise, retire.
Arise, retire.
Work and pray and dance.
Retire.

I could build a house here and let go the dream
of the swaying of camels, the saltwater lapping.

But I heard a voice—and its memory has me
stretching my neck at the dry desert wind.
Still I hear only whisper of sand and tent flapping.

Arise, retire, and I used to pray
at every new dawn, "Lord, is it today?"
Arise and retire. I no longer ask
but remain in my tent. You know I'll obey.

I'll make it my work to arise and retire
and cling to the ghost of the voice in the fire.
But, Lord, there's the ocean.
And what shall I do with this lack of motion?

Year Three, January

In the grimy daylight, snarls and snares
of strung Christmas lights strangle the trees
like barbed wire, garroting garages.

On the road home from the clinic
after another blood draw in search of
nothing in particular, in search of
everything, I watch for my
landmark, an abandoned
nativity in a roadside field:

plywood angel, plastic star.

Twenty yards beyond, a spindly camel
and three flimsy figures,
pose as if moving
toward something,
though they never reach it.

The third one stands bedraggled, farthest back,
deep in the scabby iron field.

Familiar, the way his bathrobe flaps
about him in the whining wind.

Voodoo doll, my double
in the sleet and dust, spring
approaches. Let's
one of us, at least,
last.

The Issue

(Luke 8:43-44)

When she reached, it was another
in a long series of reachings. Twelve years,
off and on, between the times she thought
she might be on the mend and the times
she gave up once again. Twelve years
of seeking corners, curling in, not
meeting eyes; twelve years of dust
in her hair, in her teeth, the dragging pull,
limp-legged wet-rag wring and chafe:
twelve years off-kilter and the crusty
dregs of a life.
The true reach
came before the jockey and scrum:
the resolve to reach once again
when it was reaching she was most sick of.
But something was different
in the air. A new color, a new
wind. She shivered in her bones
like a tree when he swept past
scouring, astringent and bright. Her neck-
hair rose. Everything about him
said, "Why not you?" Everything about him
said, "Reach with all you are. Nothing else
is worth holding onto." She leaned in.

My son's guitar class

is tucked above a carpet store
on a busy street with no parking
so that I come in panting

with the smell of traffic in my clothes,
tight-necked from the argument in the car
because this boy won't be hurried.

But, settled on a bench in the back, I
watch him bend to his patterning. Soon
the walls disappear into feathered strummings

that eddy around my ankles, pile gauzy in corners
like cottonwood. I wish I could tuck
a gentle tendril against my wrist

to pull from my sleeve and wave, a white flag,
whenever I feel my jaw clench
at this boy. He arches his neck

over the trailing crochet of music,
gazing off at something
beyond us both.

In the Locker Room at the Temple

First, in goes the coat
and her oldest's failure to get a job.
With the black shoes go
her husband's sarcasm this morning;
with her scarf goes her own.

The blouse carries the lesson
she hasn't prepared,
the dirty bathroom tile,
and the dying tree in the backyard.

Her teenager's refusal to get up
and all of those tardies
hang from her skirt like tassels.

Insidious,
gathered in the folds of her half-slip
with tentacles like clammy drier lint:
all the ways she is a terrible mother.

Her white stockings, hope
that there is another page,
another day, a horizon somewhere,
stay on her calves, enduring.

She stands a moment, shivering.

Then,
silky slip washes down her hips
like good enough.
Dress of standing straight
and facing forward.
Slippers of small things,
little graces, daily manna
that can't be hoarded
but can be found
unlooked for,
just in time.

She takes up her packet of
God's daughter
and steps out into the light.

Among the Veils

(a golden shovel*)

My hair—holding still the scent of rush, the smog and fuss from
which I've sought sanctuary—she lifts from my forehead with the
tenderness of a nurse cleansing clotted cord-blood
from a newborn. I imagine the tingle of witch-hazel and
cotton. Damp, I bow under her touch. My sins—
late-night snarls, bustle and qualm, heartburn of
peering around corners, stinginess—here in this
breezy, veiled tent of regeneration,
flake away like scales, leaving clean
tender skin: I'm new, every
fresh whit.

*   "Golden Shovel" is the name of a poetic form invented by Terrance Hayes to hon-
or poet Gwendolyn Brooks. Its distinguishing characteristic is that it takes a phrase
directly from another piece of writing (originally, a poem by Gwendolyn Brooks) and
uses each word in that phrase as the ending word for each line in the new poem.

Woman at the Well

Let me tell you. Once
on a dusty afternoon with the drop
of a bucket into a well a crack
opened in my mind:
light, air. I took
my first deep breath in years—

years of bending under burdens, the weight of what's
for dinner, the flies, the fear of a lowered brow,
of the darting of certain eyes;

I set it all down and forgot
my body for fifteen, twenty precious minutes
that were translucent, outside

time; shining moments that reminded me I had been small
once, fresh and bright and precious
to someone, needing only to trust, open
my mouth and be filled, sure that
I was, and had,
enough.

I replay that day every time I wake. Look,
now I can go through a day and a day and a day open-
mouthed like a bird,
I can remember that light.

It's important that you believe me. There is nothing so light
as was that bucket that day. I could have drawn
and drawn forever.

The sound of a whisper

is my exhale
in yoga class, which next week shivers the aspen.
Some streaming susurrus of prayers, confessions, off-stage prompts
and the answer to number four circles the sky
pricking my kitten's ears. The grass
she slinks through sings in some other field
to a lonely boy reluctant to go home.

My mother's dustcloth on the bannisters on Thursdays,
and the glide of the lotion on her hands.

The interstate breathing at dusk, five miles
from the small town where newlyweds huddle under the blanket
in his parents' house.
It's their breath. Ten years later it is their
negotiation of how to place presents under the tree.
Snow laps the window; the furnace purrs on.

My mother's sewing scissors cutting cloth for clothes
I refuse to wear.
It's a child with a dandelion, the kiss
of an orange peel pulling away, a shuffled paperback.
It's the slide of a bridal dress down hips, an old man's stroke
on an old dog, rice that my mother pours into a pot.

My hair hitting
the floor under my mother's scissors,
her corduroy and sensible shoes.

A teenaged boy with a phone number
on the way home from the dance. The record-player needle
moving beyond the last track on my mother's record; bald,
she waits in the chair.

Your breath on my ear at the end of a party: time to go.
The lonely boy steps over the cracks in the sidewalk, chanting,
and the grasses sigh to him. The old man leans into his wife
at the back of the bus to tell her something exquisite and small.

My mother directing my hands
as I wash her. I wring lukewarm water into a bowl.

Ages

4

The pony round and gentle as your mother
waits just for you against the fence
for you
and against the fence the milkweed
is bursting open just for you
and the day is endless
and the sky,
and your bed smells like your mother
like home. Other
people's houses don't smell the same.
Other people's mothers
have strange lipstick and sharp
angles, and you don't know
what is down the hall.

14

The world is all hallways
with corners. Things lead
to other things. Can't sit still, can't
quit holding your breath. Something
is coming, please
let there be something coming.
Other people's houses are so endlessly
interesting. Your mother
keeps blocking your view.
Boys are an unopened package, eyelashes
and shoulders, their fascination
with things that aren't you makes you
want them more;
they look to horizons and sleep with abandon.

24
Slow leak.
A break in your borders, endless hiss of milk and sweat
and tears. Seven pounds of baby is a universe
that blocks the sun. You disappear.
A hand on the small of your back steadies you,
eyes that catch yours across the table, across
the midnight pacing with the colicky, bruisable
piece of what was once you that you'll never
be able to keep, never
be able to let go. There is love, and
there is love, and there is a jagged
something else that leaves you white-knuckled
and panting.

34
Someone calls you "lady," as in, "Hey, lady!" and you
look around for a grown-up. You're supposed
to know something now? You missed the moment
of the passing of your prime. You feel the weight
but not the weight.
Car pools. Banking errors. Parent-teacher conferences.
You listen for the last door closing at night.
You are moving water, never arriving. Fake it.
You are here, somewhere,
in your comfortable shoes.

44

You ran into a "girl" your husband used to date,
only she was middle-aged, heavy, her roots
showing. She had bags under her eyes.
You walked away and realized that she was probably
thinking all that about you.
It's too late to specialize in anything.
Supposedly, your people are running the world.
The fear that you are turning out average.
The relief that you are turning out average. After
you give up the fight (Clairol, retinol, slimming pants),
there is the world.
The beautiful, beautiful world.

54

To look at a child when he is speaking is to rain,
gently, to seep into the cracks of things. The zip
of an orange peel is the hush of peace. All is well.
Trust the sky. Stop for the twilight and all birds.
To ignore a phone chime is to stretch out into the space
you've been given. Make room for lilac and moss.
People usually survive. You are as irritating
to your children as you were to your parents
and as dear. Enact daily festivities:
the stroking of a wrist, the lighting of a lamp.
Adults are still just as frightened, only in splinters.
Live as a semicolon: assertive,
but postponing judgment.
Water solves many things. Breathe.

From Under My Desk at James E. Moss Elementary, 1981

An alarm barks, echoing through linoleum hallways that smell
    of chalk and tater-tots. On the intercom, Mrs. Pilcher's metallic
monotone directs us to "Duck and cover. Duck and cover."

Does she practice this chant at night in her unimaginable bedroom?
    On my knees under the desk, curled into a question
mark I ponder Mrs. Pilcher, snorting and drooling on flannel at night.

Why do they have us wrap our arms around our heads if not to shut
    out this world we've inherited? The lady with the baby voice
from Archie Bunker (*bunker?*) keeps interrupting *Gilligan's Island*

with pictures of bulbous-bellied starving children. I think of the orange
    Gideon Bible the man in the grocery-store parking lot tried
to hand my mother, and how my mother wouldn't take it, would have none

of it, walking away like changing a channel in his face and so I took it,
    because who could leave a hand hanging there like that,
one holding a Bible? And his words, about the anger of God—

under my desk, I remember them. Under my desk I think
    of the day the class was full of whispers about shots.
I thought at first it was "Who shot J.R. Ewing?" again—

that old debate I couldn't participate in because *Dallas* was forbidden
    at my house, though Kimberly's mother let her watch *anything,*
and also get her ears pierced, and also wear bikinis—

but it turned out that it wasn't J.R. this time but President Reagan.
    President Reagan. Was shot. Was dead.
No, wasn't dead. Jodie Foster shot him.

No, the man who loved Jodie Foster shot him. What does
    Jodie Foster think of that? Does Jodie Foster duck and cover?
And had I sinned when I threw the Gideon bible in the garbage?

I see tender curls against the neck of the boy kneeling in front of me,
    his desk plastered with hockey stickers. Should I watch
hockey? Maybe then he'd love me, and not Kimberly. The alarm stops.

We climb back into our seats. Today I will draw a picture of a horse
    and that boy will say it's the best in the class. I will throw away
the crusts from my sandwich and think of Ethiopians

that look to me like E.T. I will play *Charlie's Angels* at recess
    and Kimberly will make me be Sabrina again,
as always. And the girl we call "Tina," who came with her family

on a boat from Thailand or Vietnam or some place
    will spend recess hiding in the giant tire again.
As always.

To Be a Girl

Pearl. A quaint preening. Better
to be wanted than to want. The sweet
hum caress
of a dress
that clings where it should,
mmm, that's good,
even better
if someone's watching,
ka-ching!
But this is not you. This
is the tender gristle
of trying,
the crossed legs of baiting, dangling

a sandal off your toe,
as if in the know. Pressing
towards arresting
after finally getting breasts.
Posed, primed, poolside,
oiled legs like wares on a cloth.
To be hunted is
to be chosen is
to be picked
like a lock
or a scab.
Enter a room with bored eyes,
hypnotize

them, never glance
down. Perky underpants,
chilly courting dance.
Envy the boys,   casual anvils:
they never pause to take a breath on the brink
of a room the easy clothes the breezy
saunter down a street never dropping the beat
no flush when a car slows nearby with maybe
fireworks, maybe death, maybe nothing. No
panties in pails, no
checking their nails.

At what age
does a girl learn to look
over her shoulder? Suck
in your gut, fight wilt,
end each statement with a lilt:
a walking question mark. The guilt
of drawing notice, of failing
to draw notice. Push,
but apologize along the way:
pardon me for living,
misgiving.
Be flashy, not brash,
make a splash
but don't dimple
the water.
Stop it.
Girl, unfurl.

Communicant

The temple: all light and air and antiseptic,
bracing, clean and brisk. All about angles,
arrows, borders and portals. I leave
feeling scoured, prickled by astringence,
spangled. Like rolling in snow after the hot tub.

But sometimes I want earth. Give me humus
and pollen, helicopter seeds, cottonwood.
Give me a close, dark den to curl in,
or a warm, amniotic night to disappear into,
translucent as I flow past lit windows
in the evening, surfing the fruity exhales
of earwigs and fitful dreamers.
I am not neat. I am blood and freckle
and cat-hair and woodgrain and flesh.
Jostle and jank, hip-yaw and shimmy.
I am nebulous, brindled and whorled.

On Sundays I juice up and digest
a piece of sky that will purge me
of my sins, and it will be delicious.
God becomes bread becomes me,
glorious and messy in its grace.

"In Sickness and in Health"

Loathe the smell
of myself, these
sheets, the constant
ragged termite whine:
I might die and
leave things undone

or, more harrowing:
I might live and leave
things undone—
a lame limb
trailing me in the dust.

Loathe the walls
and ceiling: my own body
inside out.

Love was once the lightning;
it has become the bread.

While my loathing clots
my lashes, coats
my teeth, you
still, strangely, reach
for me, this gritty
fickle prison,

stroke
between my fingers,
soft. Love holds
my hair back from my face
as I retch, appears
before me in my raging:

kind,
still.

Marriage

is the nubby recliner in the corner,
fabric dangling at an angle
from the footrest
which still works
nicely. Set next to the bed, it's
seen us through pregnancy heartburn,
colicky babies, insomnia,
recoveries in great variety. These
days it holds the things we want
near us at night: paperbacks,
breath mints, that creased
Caribbean cruise coupon. We'd
have to clear a place
if we needed to sit down
away from the bed,
which we don't, tonight.

Postpartum

Sucked dry, her ashy body flakes away.
She bows her head into the blessing blast,
the shower's braiding fingers pulling past
her ears and throat in webs of streaming gray.
The water, snaking down, gathers her tears
and curls past swollen breasts in milky flood
to swirl around her ankles with her blood:
she'll leak and melt until she disappears.
Her hands, unanchored, pass along her thighs,
her hips, her sagging womb. The pounding rain
can't wash the echoes of her baby's cries.
Young husband comes to watch through smudgy pane—
her edges blur. He squints and wonders why
she's staring, always staring at the drain.

The High Noon of Middle Age

The sour diapers of morning
give way to the overripe plums of noon
give way to the designer cheese of evening.

—Dean Young

Are these the plums that you were saving
for breakfast? Noon means
we figured out long ago
that finders are eaters
and don't leave them
in the fridge if you're not sharing. Maybe
the plums are these over-juicy
teenagers looking for rides
to the skate park. Noon means
the place of most light: a pause
between the high-heeled boots of the past
and the sweat socks of the future. It means
I care as much these days for the week
as the weekend—as good
a definition of joy as
I'm likely to find. Or still
having a little energy but knowing
what to save it for. Something good

to listen to during rush hour so
I'm no longer rushed. Noon is
knowing the summit
is around here somewhere and it doesn't
matter precisely where
anymore. Overripe plums drop
of their own accord and taste
just as sweet. Noon is
the place I catch up to myself,
panting, and begin
to look around. I'm licking
my fingers, steadying
my pulse. Noon is
finally feeling
like a person, not
a young person nor an old person.
I've still got that designer cheese
in mind, but it can wait. Noon means
I've learned how to wait
and when not to.

The Band Reunited and We All Bought Tickets

Praise God for a venue with a parking lot.

Praise God for sensible shoes and the group howl of all of us fellow boombox headphone tinnitus victims, swivel hips twinging already with intimations of mortality. For two hours we squint, wanting at once to catch each others' eyes and to hide from all the middle-aged bulges, jowls and crow's feet. This music grows our hair back and tightens our buns.

Praise God for soft-bellied musicians willing to make us sixteen again, still sleek and on the move, sure there is something exciting ahead. This voice, this song, holds everything the world promises to the young, and we will have it all, yes we will.

We smell the dance-club smoke and Polo cologne from thirty years before. We are a pack of wolves working ourselves up for the hunt, the state championship, the junior prom. We are a swarm, turning as one with the bridge of the song like a school of fish. Here, there are no mom-jeans, no dirty toilets and bosses with halitosis, unsettling lab results, finance charges. Synthesized waves of promise carry us along a river of right-this-moment; we surf on the edge of now and any-minute-now, a curl we haven't caught in thirty years.

With the wind in our faces we turn to catch each other's eyes, slapping palms: we were there! We're still here!

Hallelujah!

Depeche Mode in the Produce Section

That song. Under the fluorescents I'm feeling up
apples when I hear it, and there in my orthotics
and four-baby paunch I smell you again, you
in your pegged jeans, leather jacket
with Psychedelic Furs scrawled on the sleeve, you
sprawled on your British flag blanket—always,
even when we kissed, just out of reach,
which was half the excitement. How like you
to choose a break-up song for our "song." One hip
against the asparagus, I find I can spare
five minutes for Facebook, and there you are—
middle management, mustached! My dear,
the greatest calamity has occurred:
we've become Walmart people.
We drive carpools and suck
water from flooded basements with wet-vacs.
Those Depeche Mode boys
might be using walkers by now, drooling,
as you will someday. Those lips.

Waiting at the Airport for Her Missionary Son

Years ago, the ache was of swollen breasts
against cloth, the needles of let-down, damp and sour
when he cried. Weaning meant turning away,
letting his father hold him. Now, for two years
she has done it again, and though he is returning
she knows that she is not allowed to take him up again.
Yes, she'll throw her arms around him, feel his body
once again within the shelter of hers (aching bones,
flabby breasts and womb, old feedbag). A sip,
but nothing quenching. He is already gone.
For two years she has kept up her end
of a false umbilicus crocheted of weekly cheerful emails
(detritus of lullabyes), tatted knots of prayers, the lacework
of his own letters, beautiful and painful in their gaps.
He isn't hers. Once she went alone to an aquarium—jeweled
slivers arcing in a watery dance; in delight
she turned, searching for her child, needing to point.
There was no one to see her point.
Hypothesis: motherhood = pointing. After the cupping,

sheltering, filling, the pointing, aiming him outwards,
leading him forward, nudging
him forward, pushing
him forward, singing
him away from her. What happens
when the road leads over the horizon?
Motherhood = a journey without arrival.
The destination is the loss
of destination. Her body
slouches, bulky flattened wadding
of an old couch. She holds the mold
of the bodies that used her. Husk. Eggshell. Used
drinking glass in the sink—shatter it and plaster it
on the walls of a temple. She looks around,
doesn't know where to look. She will dissipate
into the air like a cloud passing into fair—still there,
but harder to see.

Sulphur Creek Canyon Invocation

What I want is what I've always wanted.
What I want is to be changed.

—Mary Szysbist

It isn't enough to pass through,
splashing walls like a crime scene.
How does one become a place?

Must I live a day and a day and a day
until the shade crossing the canyon
in window-blind stripes teaches me

a new rhythm: rock, pinion, coyote?
Or until the wind rubs me into nappy
velvet sandstone sponge like the red

skin of the world? Splay myself
against this stone, tack me to earth
with clothespins, this curl of creek

a scar in my skin? If I string myself
by my clavicles, an O-Kee-Pa windchime, would the whistling in my ribcage

sing me awake? Do I breathe it—
rushing, winnowing—or could it breathe me?

River, wear my scales into pearls; let
the flakes of all I've seen and been crust
the saltgrass. I will eddy until at last

I rest, a ghost in dusty drifts
against the ankles of the juniper,
borderless and wide.

Advice from the Preacher*

everything's on fire
don't be surprised
this is what's given

you might try religion
you don't need much
approach with fear and trembling
you'll sacrifice something
carry through on that promise right away
sleep soundly after a hard day's work

suffer the whims of the earth and sky
everyone has a boss
layers of inevitable bureaucracy
just more air
be still

too many worries
too many words
the more you have
the more you'll lose
appreciate what comes
the clouds that fill your dreams
you can only sit in one room at a time

when you die
don't be surprised
God, though he is willing to listen, also looks forward to silence
everyone kneels
this is what's given

---

*   All language in this poem is drawn directly from "Ecclesiastes 5" in *Nothing New Under the Sun: A Blunt Paraphrase of Ecclesiastes*, by Adam S. Miller, 2016.

On Living With a Teenager

Go softly. You are the resistance
training he'll move beyond, sweaty,
in need of a haircut. Think
like a rubber drain stop,
a traffic cone. You are what
he swerves around without seeing;
he won't see you again for years.
You missed the moment
he moved beyond you,
leaving you drinking his exhaust
like a pit crew in your dirty jumpsuit.
Pretend he is speaking English
as a Second Language.
Your protests are white noise
but so is your tenderness.
Take what you can get;
dumpster dive: the way
he watches that girl at church,
the advice you overhear him giving
a friend, the book he thinks you don't know
he stole from your shelf—all
of these are groundfruit. Pick up
what you can and lick
the juice from your fingers.

My Teenager Gets His Wisdom Teeth Out

At first, we giggle at the effects of the gas: you
mumbling and drooling through a crooked grin,
pawing at rainbows. I want a soundtrack
of 60s psychedelic. Cue the mirrored ball.

But then you get belligerent, try to stand up. Why
won't anyone let you? Batting away the nurse's hand,
you try to wedge your clumsy fist into the mouth
you cannot feel, tug on bloody gauze. You yell.

I picture now a new potential: you
as an angry drunk someday, your future
son hiding under his bed. Or dementia: you
at eighty-five, bullying a dutiful daughter-in-law.

How fragile our chemistry! Which is the real you,
the real me? How precarious our personal universe,
when one little whiff, one pulse of the button
on our chemical blender turns us beast.

I gather you up, already a foot taller than me, spitting
and thrashing like a two-year-old who hates the carseat.
My son, it is as you suspect: I'd like to strap you
somewhere safe, a padded gondola, float you

in gentle rivers for sixty years or so. It's the sin
of the fearful mother. Forgive. My chemistry names you flesh
of my flesh. But my hand warm on your arm
is a screaming offense. Ah, for now, let's just get you home.

Scrapbook

I was too much a windchime. Occasionally I flew, or melted
into the grass. Here is my bad knee, my old mouth, that tilted
back tooth. And here the air on toes after a long day's work,
the taste of mint, the scent of brakes going bad. I shared
a pillow with a kind man. I rocked sick babies in the night. I sang
to them, and to the stars; sometimes I sang to
raise the roof and felt wings brush my cheeks.
I wore mom-jeans. Here is dappled shade. Here is faraway
weeping. Here is the close-up weeping that I could hold, and some
that I couldn't. I shook hands and licked pennies and cleared
my throat and looked away. I checked tires and removed
makeup and apologized. I dropped the subject. I took a breath.
There were earaches and pinkeye, milk and good bread
and raspberries. I voted and failed to vote. I listened to busy
signals. Here is a crack in the driveway; here that phonecall.
I intended something. I intended something else. I ate chocolate.
Here is an ad, and another ad, and another ad. I missed
a beat. I didn't sleep. I waited. I thirsted; I fasted, I stared
at ceilings; I snored. Here is the scent of my mother's nightgown.
Here, a clogged gutter. I gained weight. I paid bills. I turned
my cheek towards a long twilight. Here is a long line
at customer service, a dollar movie, childbirth stirrups.
Here is the shush of temple robes; here the cry of a cat alone
on a cold night. There was everything; there was cut grass
and used car lots and baby quail under the lilacs. It was
all. It was enough.

Release and Sustaining

Just three years ago, I stood like you,
smiling shyly, staring straight ahead,
whispers on my neck. I gripped the pew,
a little dizzy as my name was read.
Now you stand. A circuit switch is thrown.
The shock of silence where there once was hum
deflates me. I'm vestigial, left to mourn
the sweet, familiar current. Empty, numb,
I am a husk, a glove without a hand.
I am sloughed skin, a tree with no more fruit.
I sit bereaved while, innocent, you stand
already blossoming as you take root.
The bright charge snaps and sparks about your hair.
I raise my right hand, empty in the air.

Umbilical Cord

Yes, press your hand against my flesh to feel
this fresh-bright life, this future man of God
flex tiny stretching legs to test the walls
of a quart-sized world of warm and wet.

All life he drinks direct through twisted cord,
source of constant nourishment through me;
fast it holds, despite his testing squirms,
building a defense from future harm.

There! Your palm is humming from his kick
But now you move away and fall asleep . . .

Soon your hands will press against his head
while I pray empty-bellied on a pew.
Flesh on flesh, you'll make the cord of life,
antibody strength for future fights—

may it hold fast.

Mastitis

Anna's baby wouldn't eat, and so the angels gathered.
Her mother Jo, gone by cancer three years now.
Her aunt Emily, also cancer, fifteen years.
Her great, great, great grandmamma Susan, whom she'd
never met on earth, but who had been her best
friend in heaven (duets, giggles, spying
on other ancestors) headed up the effort, drew up
schedules, chaired the committee meetings. Paul,
destined to be Anna's third-born in about six years,
was assigned to the machines: dishwasher, car,
furnace; he saw to it that nothing broke, each
to fulfill its measured purpose. Sadie, Anna's
future eldest granddaughter, made sure birds sang
each morning, which Anna could hear when she
stopped crying long enough to make herself breathe.
Grandma Susan whispered to the baby. "Remember,
remember," she said. "We promised it would be short.
It gets better. We're still near. Good things are coming."
Mother Jo, able to dip in and out of time as they all were,
braided memories of cradling Anna herself—
kissing her palms, her inner elbows, the soles
of her feet, as she now gentled her grown girl,
stroking her hair, her back ("strength in the spine,
strength in the spine," she chanted). Sometimes
she sang her lullabies. "I am here. I am here.
You are strong. You can do this. You are all
you need to be, my love. All, my love."

This Pleasant Bench

There are girls on campus
wearing plaid shirts with striped pants,
and I've become my mother,
of the sensible shoes, well on my way
to becoming my grandmother,
of the elastic-waist polyester pants.
Already I've learned the value
of an early dinner. I begin
to see the old women,
the ones sitting small in corners, serene.
It's not that they don't dare
drive faster; it's that their lives
have caught up with them.
No "buffering" while the game loads.
Sister Wardall always sat on the back row
in our discussion group, smiling with her eyes
while we young mothers worked hard to hack
out a place in the world with words,
our plexiglass hatchets.

I know now what she was thinking:
yes, yes, be passionate. But sitting down
is nice, too.
We were on our feet fighting
and she was holding our babies for us,
quietly saving the world
a little, finishing up in time
for a nap. As my eyes get older
the line begins to blur between
saving the world and savoring it.
Who is it you're dressing for, pretty
young thing in the giant
boots and pants like pantyhose? Yes,
take it seriously, all of it.
But I'll smile someday
when you join me on my
pleasant bench.

One Day at the Temple, I Forget the Words

Twenty-five years I've been coming to this place,
doing these things, saying
these words. They are as familiar
as my own fingernails (the crooked pinkie),
keeping me company, these words, during achingly
ordinary days, winging down from trees,
a flutter just at the edge of sight.
Some days they spark, fireflies. Or
bob, pale bubbles, adrift. Or preside,
like bricks, toe-stubbers. An extension
cord connecting me to another dimension,
quantum entanglement, if the conditions
are right. Today, they're not.

Blame the weather. Blame the slammed door
yesterday, other words thrown
over a shoulder. The headache,
the run in the stocking. All the things I forgot
to leave in the locker, maybe. Mind
too full to carry the words
that should be carrying me.
Never mind. Angels wait nearby,
eager to whisper, eager to hand me along,
loving me more for needing their help.
I will sit in this place and empty myself
of all the words. There is nowhere else to go.

Pantoum for Mary at the Tomb

(after Why Weepest Thou?, a painting by J. Kirk Richards)

Her weeping is the only sound; the birds hold their breath.
What's missing, what she fears, this is all she can think.
She has her back to Him. If only she would turn around.
Curled in on herself, she perches between light and

what's missing. What she fears is all. She can think
her arm braces her, but it blocks her progress,
curled in as she is on herself, perched between dark and
the light which, coming from above, catches both aslant.

She braces herself, but her arm blocks her progress.
We observe from ground level. We know the secret.
We see through the light from above that catches both aslant:
He is there, endlessly patient.

Observing from ground level, we know the secret:
this is the moment just before the moment of what matters;
He is there, endlessly patient.
He waits for her to turn her face to the future before he calls to her.

In this moment just before the moment of what matters,
the sun is climbing. The shadow on His face will withdraw
as he waits for her to turn her face to the future. Before he calls
    to her,
his face, though hidden, is bent toward her.

As the sun climbs, the shadow over His face will withdraw.
His palms are open; surely comfort is there.
His face, though hidden, is bent toward her.
He is about to call her name.

He stands with comfort in His open palms;
I want to tell her to turn around. Maybe
He is about to call her name, and then
all shall be well, and all shall be well.

I want to tell her to turn around. Maybe
it's His love for her, in her pain, that makes Him pause.
All shall be well, and all manner of thing shall be well,
but we are all, each, stuck in this moment.

Perhaps in his pauses, in our pain, there is love for us.
If she could stop weeping, she might hear the birds.
Everyone alive is stuck in this moment.
I want to turn around.

Gethsemane

I want to tell the story. But—
there is no approaching this,
strange crux
of everything.

Come at it sideways.
Come at it from the edge.

Picture, then,
a hardscrabble patch of land.
Rocks. An olive tree. Sparse,
straggling desert grass. The rocks

have been waiting. The wind
has been waiting. The living souls nearby
sleep through the whole thing.
(This is important. I have slept
through many things.)

And then—
What

can be known? There has never been
any moment more private
nor more public.

So.
What I know: the screaming windy cliff
of unavoidable onus, the weight
of what must be done.
For me, it was the abyss
of being about to give birth. The way
the self shrinks
to a pinpoint in a vacuum, the way
one becomes lost, faceless,

the way
the thought that there is another soul depending on you
can pull you inside out and through
to a new place.

But of course
even in that, my most impossible moment,
he was already there,
having been there before me.

Oh, how is a human
to comprehend godly heartbreak?
Might as well teach a point on a line
about temples and spires,
about stars. It's a matter of dimension:
impossible geometry.

What we know:
he went to a place.
He knew that ahead of him
was a pain yet unknown in the world,

extra-dimensional. That
seeing it, he, who had maybe
never known fear before this,
asked to be excused,
but not really.

We know:
the contemplation of that pain
was so terrible it required the ministration
of an angel before it could be approached.

We know:
at point zero
he was left alone
in a way no human can comprehend.

We know:
he came out on the other side
gentle, generous,
quieter.

Forever after,
he would say very little about it.
Only: *shrink.*
Only: *nevertheless.*

Joseph and the "Ladder-Day Saints"

It's what I, as a kid, thought our name was, and, really,
    is it so inaccurate? I don't care
whether he *found* the ladder
    (dust, spade sparking on flint),
built the ladder
    (sawdust, fittings and frame),
or *received* it from the hands of a blazing angel
    (squint, tremble, sear)—

because of him, I'll never be stuck deep in the hole
    of believing this is all there is,
    all there ever will be.

Born just when the world was getting good at forward motion,

    he taught height.

Heaven isn't a place; it's a verb.
    Damnation is simply a lack of progress.
        There is no outside curtain.
            Worlds without number; works without end.
                For ladder days unceasing,
                    we're on the up and up.

Prayer

> *I like it when you jerk*
> *the reins I know the gee or haw*
> *if either comes will come from you*
>
> *—Maurice Manning*

From inside my Walmart-colored cave
my neck is aching from the looking up.
A heartsick earwig snuffling out your scent,
I've lost the trail, the recipe. I Google you.
You're out of reach but stuck between my teeth.
I check the rearview mirror, sift through spoons.
Can't shake the feeling that's your trailing sleeve
I glimpse in the "Check Engine Soon" light, your wink
in the tender inner elbow of my son.
I toss this crumpled paper bag of prayer
hoping you'll catch. Yoo-hoo? Please, pretty please,
take the reins and hie me off to Kolob. Slap
me upside my intentions, whatever it takes:
sock me holy sweetly in the jaw.

Acknowledgments

Thanks to the following publications in which these pieces previously appeared, sometimes in a slightly different version:

Atlanta Review ("To a Red Traffic Light")
BYU Studies ("Horizon," "My Son's Guitar Class")
Dialogue ("Echo of Boy")
Ellipsis ("In Sickness and in Health")
Fire in the Pasture: 20th Century Mormon Peculiar Pages, 2011
     ("Angels of Mercy," "How Long?," "Postpartum")
Irreantum ("Digestion in the Garden," "How Long?," "Postpartum,"
     "Umbilical Cord," and "Release and Sustaining")
The Mother in Me, Deseret Book 2008 ("Umbilical Cord")
River Teeth ("The Band Reunited and We All Bought Tickets")
Seasons of Change, Segullah 2017 ("How Long?," "Horizon")
Segullah ("Shepherds")
Victorian Violets ("Postpartum")
Wisconsin Review ("From Under My Desk at James E. Moss
     Elementary, 1981," "Salt")

Gratitude to Harlow Clark, past poetry editor of *Irreantum*, who first gave me a place to write for an audience, and to the entire Association for Mormon Letters community for helping me believe that Mormons (OK, members of the Church of Jesus Christ of Latter-Day Saints) are worth writing for. Thanks to Carol Lynn Pearson and Angela Hallstrom for showing me it could be done. Thanks to Kathryn Lynard and the other women at *Segullah* for giving LDS women a place to explore questions in the context of faith. Thanks to Lance Larsen and Susan Howe for pushing me. Gratitude, of course, for Steve Evans and Michael Austin at BCC Press for taking a chance on me, and to Mikey Brooks for the beautiful cover and Andrew Heiss for expert typesetting. Thanks to my father for asking for more. Most of all, thanks to my best friend and sweetheart who sacrifices so much to support me, from those "evenings off" during our starving-student, young parenthood days to buying me my first laptop "just for writing." No one else will ever understand the extent of his selflessness. I am so blessed.

DARLENE YOUNG served as poetry editor for *Dialogue: A Journal of Mormon Thought* and for *Segullah*. She also served as secretary for the Association for Mormon Letters. She received her MFA from Brigham Young University, where she now teaches Creative Writing. She lives in South Jordan, Utah with her husband and sons.

CPSIA information can be obtained
at www.ICGtesting.com
Printed in the USA
FSHW021939201219
65342FS